First Facts™

American Symbols

The Pentagon

by Terri DeGezelle

Consultant:
Professor Gordon Adams, Ph.D.
Director, Security Policy Studies
Elliott School of International Affairs
The George Washington University, Washington, D.C.

Capstone press

Mankato, Minnesota

First Facts is published by Capstone Press
151 Good Counsel Drive, P.O. Box 669, Mankato, Minnesota 56002
www.capstonepress.com

Library of Congress Cataloging-in-Publication Data
DeGezelle, Terri, 1955–
    The Pentagon / by Terri DeGezelle.
    p. cm.—(American symbols)
    Contents: Fast facts—American symbol of defense—One building needed—Building the
Pentagon—The Department of Defense—The Pentagon attacked—The Pentagon today.
    ISBN 0-7368-2530-4 (hardcover)
    1. Pentagon (Va.)—Juvenile literature. [1. Pentagon (Va.)] I. Title. II. Series: American
    symbols (Mankato, Minn.)
UA26.A745D44 2004
355.6'0973—dc21   2003010800

Editorial Credits
Amanda Doering, editor; Linda Clavel, series designer; Molly Nei, book designer and
    illustrator; Kelly Garvin and Scott Thoms, photo researchers; Eric Kudalis and Karen
    Risch, product planning editors

The Pentagon building has been repaired since the events of September 11, 2001, and looks
    nearly identical to its original condition. Some photos in this book were taken before
    September 11, 2001.

Photo Credits
AP/Wide World Photos, 12–13, 16; Corbis/Morton Beebe, cover; Corbis/Reuters
NewMedia Inc., 14–15; Corbis Sygma/Greg Baldwin, 17; Folio Inc./Borkoski, 6–7; Folio
Inc./Davidson, 5, 19; National Archives and Records Administration, Records of the Public
Buildings Service, 20; Photo courtesy of U.S. Army Corps of Engineers, Office of History, 9,
11, 18

Table of Contents

Pentagon Fast Facts

⭐ The Pentagon is the world's largest office building.

⭐ The Pentagon has five sides and five floors.

⭐ Along each outside wall of the Pentagon, 7.5 football fields could be lined up end to end.

⭐ The Pentagon cost more than $80 million to build.

⭐ More than 23,000 people work at the Pentagon.

⭐ The Pentagon was built .75 mile (1.2 kilometers) south of its original plan. It was moved so the Pentagon would not block the view of Arlington Cemetery from the White House.

⭐ The Pentagon has 17.5 miles (28 kilometers) of hallways.

American Symbol of Defense

The Pentagon is a **symbol** of national **defense**. Many of the 23,000 workers at the Pentagon are part of the U.S. **Armed Forces**. The armed forces are part of the Department of Defense. This department helps protect the United States' freedom.

 Fun Fact:
The U.S. Armed Forces are made up of the army, navy, air force, marine corps, and coast guard.

One Building Needed

In 1941, the United States entered World War II (1939–1945). At that time, the U.S. War Department was spread out over the Washington, D.C., area.

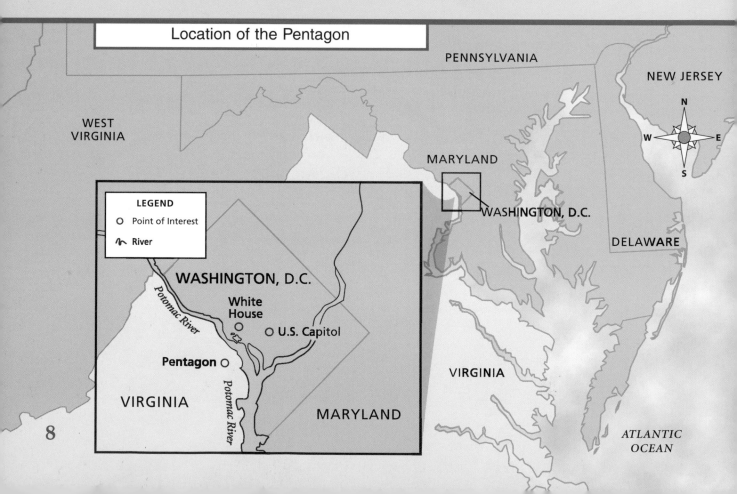

Location of the Pentagon

LEGEND
O Point of Interest
~ River

WASHINGTON, D.C.

White House

O U.S. Capitol

Potomac River

Pentagon O

VIRGINIA

Potomac River

MARYLAND

PENNSYLVANIA

NEW JERSEY

N
W   E
S

WEST VIRGINIA

MARYLAND

WASHINGTON, D.C.

DELAWARE

VIRGINIA

ATLANTIC OCEAN

The U.S. War Department needed one building for all its workers. Brigadier General Brehon B. Sommervell asked for a building. **Congress** agreed.

Building the Pentagon

Congress made plans to build in Arlington, Virginia. Construction began September 11, 1941. The Pentagon was built quickly. Some days, people worked all day and all night. The Pentagon was finished January 15, 1943.

🔍 Fun Fact:

Workers dug up sand and gravel from the Potomac River to make concrete for the Pentagon.

The Department of Defense

The Department of Defense meets at the Pentagon. The department makes decisions on how to defend the United States. The Department of Defense gives orders to the armed forces in the field. They tell the armed forces where to go and what to do.

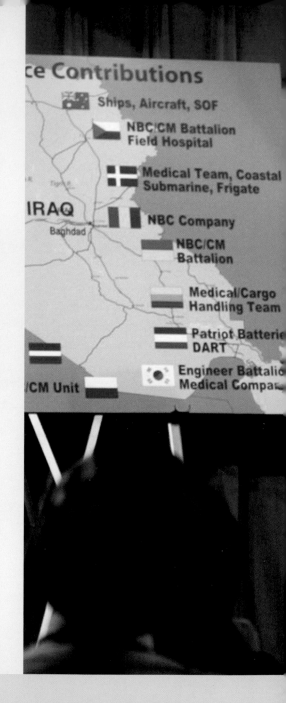

 Fun Fact:
The Department of Defense holds meetings with news reporters to inform them of what the armed forces are doing.

The Pentagon Attacked

On September 11, 2001, the Pentagon was attacked. **Terrorists** crashed a plane into the Pentagon. The plane exploded and set the building on fire. One side of the Pentagon was badly damaged. The crash killed 184 people.

 Fun Fact:
The Pentagon was attacked exactly 60 years after construction on the building began.

The Pentagon Today

Today, the damaged side of the
Pentagon is rebuilt. A **memorial** for the
people who died is planned. People
will never forget September 11, 2001.

Many people guard the Pentagon.
Only certain groups of people are allowed
to visit. The U.S. government wants to
keep this symbol of defense safe.

Time Line

September 11, 1941—
Construction starts on
the Pentagon.

July, 1941—Brigadier
General Brehon B.
Sommervell requests
a building for the
War Department.

January 15, 1943—Construction is
completed on the Pentagon.

May 17, 1976—The Pentagon Tour Program is created.

September 11, 2001—Terrorists crash a plane into the west side of the Pentagon.

September 11, 2002—Workers move back into the rebuilt area of the Pentagon.

The Pentagon got its shape from its original site. Four roads surrounded the building's site. Builders thought a pentagon shape would make the best use of the land. Later, the Pentagon site was moved south. Builders kept the original pentagon-shaped plan.

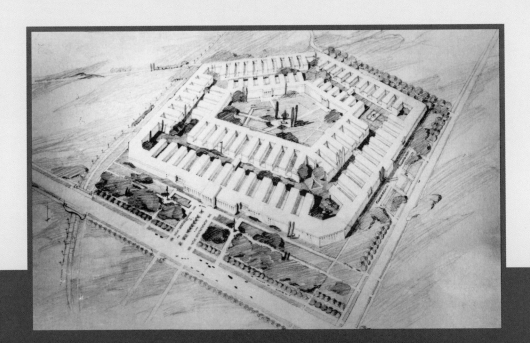

Hands On: Make the Pentagon

Pentagons have five sides. You can make a Pentagon model with straws.

What You Need

5 5-foot (1.5-meter) pieces of string
25 plastic drinking straws
scissors
white glue

What You Do

1. Thread one piece of string through five straws.
2. Lay the straws out on a flat surface.
3. Tie the ends of the string together so the first and the last straw meet. Snip off the leftover ends of the string. You should have a pentagon shape.
4. Repeat steps 1–3 to make four more pentagons.
5. Glue each pentagon on top of the other. Each layer of straws represents one floor of the Pentagon.
6. Look around the room. Do you see any other pentagons?

Glossary

armed forces (ARMD FORSS-ez)—the people who protect a country; in the United States, the branches of the armed forces include the army, navy, air force, marine corps, and the coast guard.

Congress (KONG-griss)—the branch of the U.S. government that makes laws

defense (duh-FENSS)—a protection against harm

memorial (muh-MOR-ee-uhl)—something that is built or done to remember a person or event

symbol (SIM-buhl)—an object that stands for something else

terrorist (TER-ur-ist)—someone who uses violence and threats in order to get something from a group of people or government

Read More

Britton, Tamara L. *The Pentagon.* Symbols, Landmarks, and Monuments. Edina, Minn.: Abdo, 2003.

Gard, Carolyn. *The Attack on the Pentagon on September 11, 2001.* Terrorist Attacks. New York: Rosen, 2003.

Internet Sites

FactHound offers a safe, fun way to find Internet sites related to this book. All of the sites on FactHound have been researched by our staff.

Here's how:
1. Visit *www.facthound.com*
2. Type in this special code **0736825304** for age-appropriate sites. Or enter a search word related to this book for a more general search.
3. Click on the **Fetch It** button.

FactHound will fetch the best sites for you!

Index